TIME

BRENDA WALPOLE

Photographs by Chris Fairclough
Illustrations by Dennis Tinkler

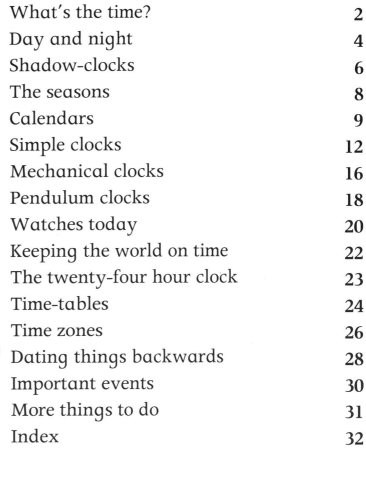

Contents

A & C Black · London

What's the time?

If someone asks you the time, what do you do? Perhaps you glance at your wrist watch, or a clock on the wall, or the time-display on a video recorder. Do you know how many different kinds of clocks and watches there are in your home?

Two hundred years ago, few people had clocks and watches of their own. People who lived in the country got up at sunrise and went to bed after sunset. In towns, people divided their days into times for eating, working and sleeping.

Today we depend on clocks to make sure we run our lives on time. During one day, make a list of all the times you use a clock to check the time.

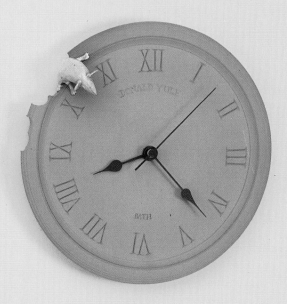

Days are divided into hours and minutes so we can measure how long it takes to do things and to make sure we do them on time. How long does it take you to travel to school or to run fifty metres?

As well as measuring short periods of time, we need to measure much longer periods of time too. How old are you? See if you can work out your age in days and hours. Do you know when your school was built? Some periods of time are too long to be measured in hours and minutes so we use months, years and centuries.

These stones have been standing for over three millennia. Find out how many years are in one millennium.

Day and night

If you had been alive before clocks and watches were invented, you would have learned to tell the time by looking at the position of the Sun in the sky.

The Sun is at the centre of our Solar System and it gives us our day and night. At any moment, one half of the Earth faces the Sun and is lit by the Sun's rays. On this side of the world it is daytime. On the opposite side of the Earth, where sunlight does not reach, it is night.

The Earth spins slowly all the time, but we don't feel any movement because it turns smoothly and at the same speed. It spins on its axis, which is an imaginary line passing through the North and South Poles. The Earth takes a whole day to make a complete turn. Long ago, people decided to divide each day into twenty-four hours.

Make day and night

You will need: a darkened room, a globe, a bright light — this stands for the Sun, a small plasticine model of a person.

Stick the model on to the globe near to where you live. Shine the light on to the globe, near the equator. Slowly turn the globe eastward. The model will see sunrise, then daylight, then sunset and then night.

What do you notice about the shadow of the model?

As the Earth spins, the Sun appears to move across the sky. Day begins when the Sun rises above the horizon in the East, and by midday it is high up in the sky. Day ends when the Sun falls below the horizon in the West.

Never look directly at the Sun because it can damage your eyes. Shield your eyes with your hand and look to the side of the Sun.

Can you tell the time from the position of the Sun in these pictures? If you cover up the Sun, are there any other clues which help you to guess what time of day it is?

5

Shadow-clocks

As the Earth spins, shadows cast by the Sun change length and direction. When the Sun is high in the sky, shadows are short and when the Sun is low in the sky, shadows are long.

The earliest known clocks used shadows to tell the time. It's thought that the ancient Egyptians built huge stone needles to use as shadow-clocks. This Egyptian stone needle is called Cleopatra's Needle.

Something to try

Make your own shadow-clock

You will need: an old broom handle stuck in a bucket of soil and stones, chalk.

Find a place outside which will be in sunshine all day. In the morning, set up your shadow-clock; mark the position and length of the shadow made by the broom handle and note the time. Take readings from your shadow-clock every hour. What happens?

Look in the newspaper for the times of sunrise and sunset and work out the time exactly half way between the two. This time is the middle of the day when the shadow on your shadow-clock should be at its shortest.

P.S. Take readings from your shadow-clock once a month for a year. What happens to the shadows?

Many parks and gardens have a different kind of shadow-clock, called a sundial. On most sundials a triangular pointer called a gnomon casts a shadow on to a flat base, which is marked with a scale of hours and minutes. Can you think of any times when shadow-clocks might not work?

The seasons

At the same time as the Earth is spinning on its axis through day and night, it is also travelling all the way round the Sun in a path called an orbit. The time this journey takes is called one solar year.

The Earth's axis is not perfectly upright so first one half of the Earth, then the other tilts towards the Sun. The Earth's axis is always tilted the same way, but because the Earth moves around the Sun, different parts of the Earth face the Sun at different times. This makes the seasons – summer, autumn, winter and spring.

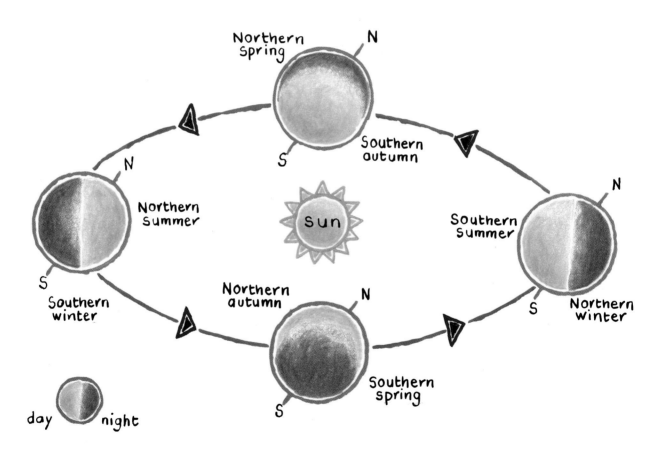

For some months of the year, the North Pole is tilted towards the Sun and the South Pole is tilted away. During this time, it is summer in the Northern Hemisphere, with long warm days, and winter in the Southern Hemisphere, with short cold days. When the Northern Hemisphere is tilted away from the Sun, it is winter there and summer in the Southern Hemisphere.

Calendars

When people began to make the first calendars they used the regular appearance of the Sun and the Moon in the sky. They noticed that a new moon changed into a full moon in about fifteen days, then back into a new moon in another fifteen. We now know that during this time the Moon orbits Earth. The time this journey takes is called one lunar month. Look at the picture. During its orbit, the Moon appears to change its shape as different parts of its surface are lit by the Sun.

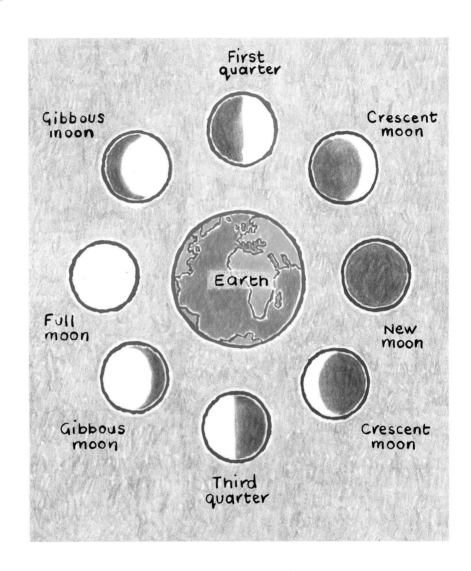

The ancient Egyptians kept records of the changes of the seasons and the stars in the sky because they wanted to know the right time to plant and harvest their crops. They worked out that a solar year was about 365 days and that twelve lunar months were about 354 days, eleven days shorter than a solar year. This meant that a calendar of twelve lunar months would soon be out of step with the seasons. The Egyptians used a calendar with twelve months of thirty days and added an extra five days at the end of each year.

9

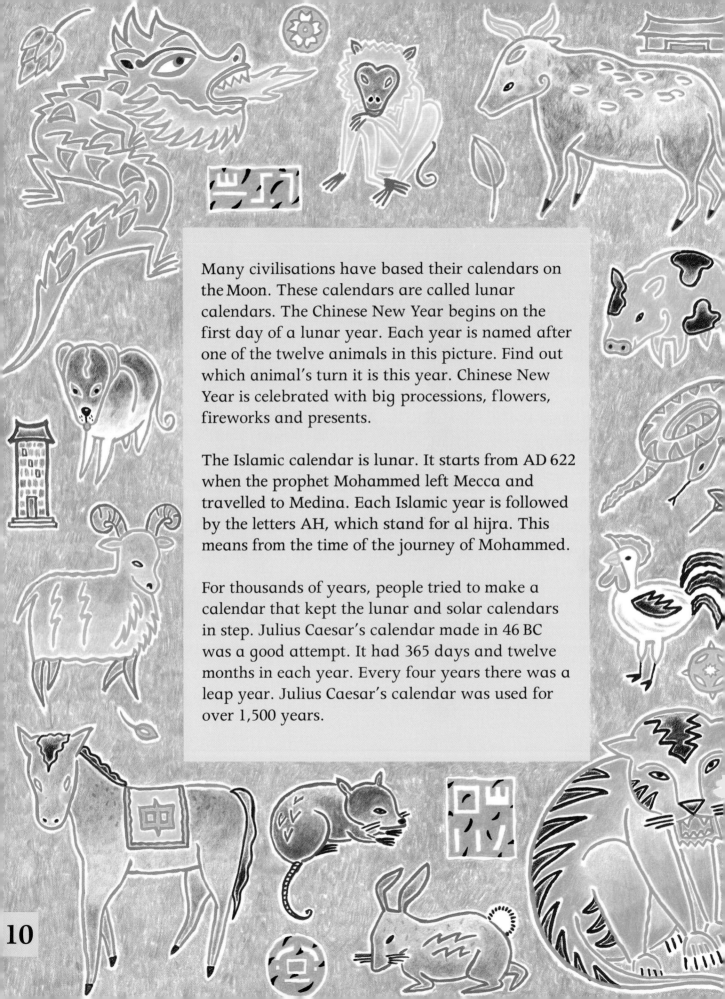

Many civilisations have based their calendars on the Moon. These calendars are called lunar calendars. The Chinese New Year begins on the first day of a lunar year. Each year is named after one of the twelve animals in this picture. Find out which animal's turn it is this year. Chinese New Year is celebrated with big processions, flowers, fireworks and presents.

The Islamic calendar is lunar. It starts from AD 622 when the prophet Mohammed left Mecca and travelled to Medina. Each Islamic year is followed by the letters AH, which stand for al hijra. This means from the time of the journey of Mohammed.

For thousands of years, people tried to make a calendar that kept the lunar and solar calendars in step. Julius Caesar's calendar made in 46 BC was a good attempt. It had 365 days and twelve months in each year. Every four years there was a leap year. Julius Caesar's calendar was used for over 1,500 years.

Julius Caesar's calendar was about eleven minutes longer than a solar year. And by 1580, the calendar was ten days out of step with the seasons. In 1582, Pope Gregory ordered the ten days to be removed. In Roman Catholic Europe, the date jumped straight from the 5th of October to the 15th October. But in Protestant England, Pope Gregory's calendar was not accepted until 1751, by which time eleven days had to be removed. Many people felt cheated and there were riots. William Hogarth painted this picture in about 1754. It is called 'Give us back our eleven days' and shows people protesting at the loss of days.

Pope Gregory's calendar was also more accurate because it stated that there would not be leap years in century years, for example the years 1700 or 1800, unless the century could be divided by 400, such as the years 1600 or 2000.

Today, many countries use Pope Gregory's calendar. It starts from the year Christians think Jesus Christ was born. Years before Christ are called BC, or 'before Christ', and years after, AD, or 'anno Domini', which is Latin for in the year of our Lord.

Simple clocks

Water-clocks

The steady flow of water can be used to measure time. The ancient Greek word for a water-clock is clepsydra, which means water thief.

Something to try

Make some water-clocks

You will need *for the sinking water-clock:*
a large bowl of water, a small plastic container which can be punctured, small balls of plasticine; a stopwatch, scissors, pen and paper.

For the dripping water-clock: a large plastic bottle with a screw top cap, a stopwatch, scissors, pen and paper, water.

For the *sinking water-clock*, pierce the base of the container and float it on the water. How long does it take for the container to sink? Try the experiment again, but this time put plasticine weights in the container. Try and make a time scale for the side of your clock.

For the *dripping water-clock*, cut the bottle in half and pierce a hole in its cap. Turn the top half of the bottle upside down and place in the bottom half. Pour water through the top. Every 30 seconds mark the rising water level on a scale.

P.S. Try and make a water-clock that measures 15 minutes exactly.

This ancient Egyptian water-clock has sloping sides which help to make the water flow evenly.

Sand-clocks

This sand-clock was made in the sixteenth century. For thousands of years, sand-clocks have been used to measure short periods of time. They were used in churches and homes, and on board ships.

Make your own sand-clock

You will need: two small empty plastic bottles of the same size, a screw top cap, scissors, salt or sand, strong sticky tape, a stopwatch.

Make a small hole in the cap and screw on to one bottle. Half fill the other bottle with salt. Put the empty bottle on top and carefully tape the bottles together.

Turn the sand-clock upside down and time how long it takes for the salt to come through.

P.S. How can you make a sand-clock that measures longer periods of time?

Candle-clocks

One story says that King Alfred invented the candle-clock in AD 870. He divided a 30 centimetre long candle into twelve sections, and it took one hour for three sections to burn down. The candle-clock was kept in a lantern to stop it blowing out in the wind.

Make a candle-clock

Ask an adult to help you make the candle-clock. Never lean over a lit candle and always blow out candles when you have finished with them.

You will need: two tall candles, a knife, a pen, a ruler, matches, a metal candle holder, a watch.

Stand one candle in the holder. Ask an adult to light the candle. Let the candle burn for half an hour, blow it out and leave the wick to cool. Measure how much the candle has burnt down against the unburnt candle. Mark off the unburnt candle into sections of this length. Now you can use the marked candle as a clock.

14

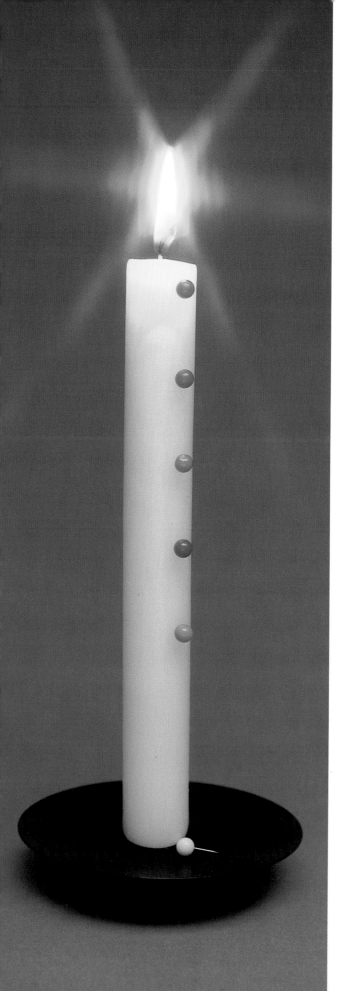

To make a candle-alarm-clock, place a metal pin on each of the marks. Ask an adult to light the candle. After the candle has burnt for half an hour, the pin will drop with a ping on to the metal holder.

P.S. Try and make a candle-alarm-clock that pings after 45 minutes.

Some candle-clocks, sand-clocks, and sinking and dripping water-clocks can be very accurate at measuring how much time has passed, but after a short while they stop. This Chinese water-clock uses the force of water to slowly turn a wheel. Then the wheel turns a timer. The water is used again and again, which means the clock can measure longer periods of time.

Mechanical clocks

Over a thousand years ago, the first mechanical clocks were made. They had no hands but instead they had bells which rang on the hour. The word clock probably comes from the Latin word for bell, clocca. This clock at Salisbury Cathedral, England, is over six hundred years old.

Early clocks used the power of a falling weight to make the mechanism turn. The weight was attached to a rope wound round a drum. As the weight fell, the drum turned and the rope unwound. The drum was connected to a toothed wheel called a crown wheel, which made the bells ring. Once a day, the rope was rewound.

Something to try

Make a falling weight drum

You will need: a pole, a cardboard inner tube, a length of string, a ball of plasticine, sellotape.

Tape one end of the string to the tube and tie the other end round the plasticine. Feed the pole through the tube. Wind the string around the tube. Hold the pole and let go of the tube and plasticine. What happens when you try this experiment with longer and shorter pieces of string and bigger and smaller pieces of plasticine?

In later clocks, hour and minute hands were connected to the crown wheels by a series of small gear wheels.

Make gear wheels for your own clock face

You will need: two jam jar lids, one slightly smaller than the other, corrugated paper, strong glue, paper fasteners, scissors, a paper clock face and hour hand, a shallow box.

Pierce a hole through the centre of each lid. Stick strips of corrugated paper round the rims. Be careful not to squash the ridges – they will be the teeth of the gears.

Attach the hand to the clock face with a paper fastener and fix through the front of the box to the big gear wheel. Use a paper fastener to fix the little gear wheel next to the big one. Make sure the wheels touch otherwise they won't turn. Paste down the clock face to the box.

What happens when you turn the small gear wheel? How far does the big wheel turn when the small wheel turns once?

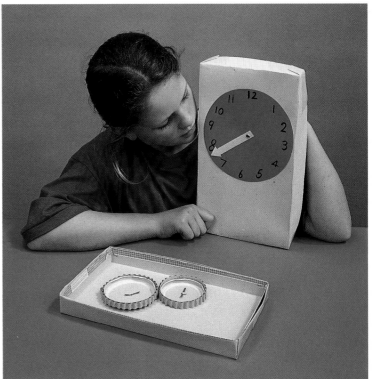

Pendulum clocks

In 1584, an Italian mathematician called Galileo watched a chandelier swinging in a draught over the altar in Pisa Cathedral. He measured the time it took for the chandelier to make one complete swing. He found that whether the chandelier swung a long way or a short way, it took the same amount of time to get back to where it started.

A pendulum is a rod with a weight called a bob attached to its end, and just like the chandelier a pendulum swings at a regular rate.

Something to try

Make a pendulum

You will need: a length of string, some plasticine, a pole, two chairs, a stopwatch.

Tie one end of the string to the plasticine and the other end to the pole. Rest the pole over two chairs. Start the pendulum swinging and time thirty double swings. Start with a big swing and then make a small one. What happens when you change the weight of the bob or the length of the string?

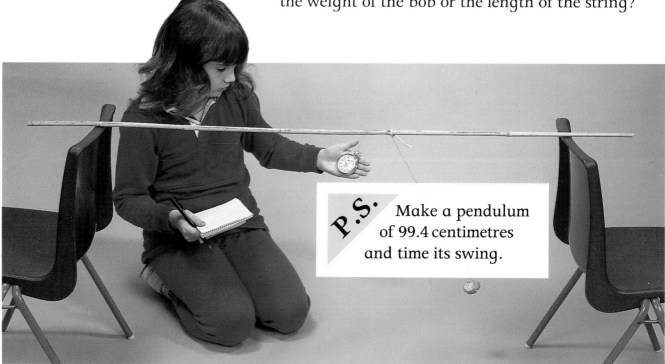

P.S. Make a pendulum of 99.4 centimetres and time its swing.

Galileo discovered how the pendulum worked but he never made a pendulum clock. In 1657, a Dutch scientist called Christian Huygens built the first pendulum clock. Clocks with long pendulums are often called grandfather clocks. Many grandfather clocks have long cases to protect the pendulum. Big Ben in London has a pendulum which is 4 metres long.

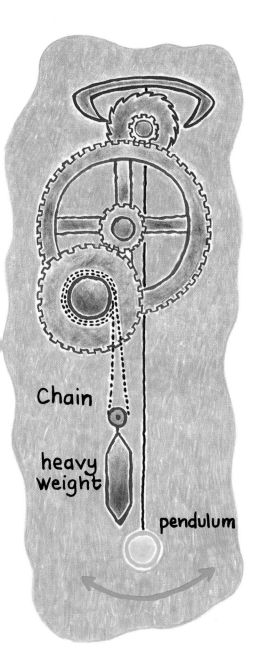

Chain

heavy weight

pendulum

A grandfather clock is powered by a chain wound round a reel. A heavy weight at the end of the chain gradually pulls the reel round. The chain is connected to a series of gear wheels, similar to the ones you made on page 17, which turn the hands. The regular swing of the pendulum stops the weight falling too quickly. Each time the pendulum swings, a bit of the chain is released and the weight falls slowly. Each week, the weight is lifted up again by the use of a winding key.

Watches today

Today many people wear watches on their wrists but in the fifteenth century watches were carried in pockets. They were beautifully decorated with gemstones and gold but they weren't very accurate.

A pocket watch had a coiled spring, called the main spring, which provided the power to turn the hands. Make a coil from thick paper and pin it to a board. What happens when you let go of the end? Pocket watches had to be wound up regularly to recoil the spring.

Modern spring-driven watches are more accurate than the early pocket watches. Inside, many have 'jewels' which help to stop the parts rubbing against one another, and make the mechanism turn more smoothly. Look on the face of an old watch to see if it has any jewels.

Most modern watches are powered by quartz crystals. Inside a quartz watch, an electric current from a small battery makes the tiny quartz crystal vibrate an exact number of times each second. Microchip parts count the vibrations and send signals to change the time-display. The microchips can count the vibrations for long enough to give a display of days and months.

Timing-computers can measure the time an athlete takes to run a race to within one hundredth of a second. When the starting-pistol is fired, a timing-counter begins. Then as the athletes cross the finishing-line, an electronic camera takes a photograph, which can be used with the timer to calculate almost exactly when each athlete crossed the finishing-line.

Keeping the world on time

Even today, we don't always use a clock or watch to tell us when it's time to do things. A prayer call from a minaret (the tower on a mosque) tells Moslems when it's time to pray. And some churches ring bells on Sundays and celebration days. The Jewish sabbath begins on a Friday at sunset.

When most people lived in the country and worked outside, it wasn't important for everyone to be able to do things at the same time, but as more people moved into towns, their lives had to become more co-ordinated.

In the nineteenth century, when the first big factories were built, few people had watches of their own. Factories sounded loud hooters to tell people when to finish work. Can you find the hooter in this picture? Children were called to lessons by a big bell. Important buildings such as churches, stations and town halls had big clocks for everyone to see.

The twenty-four hour clock

If someone arranges to meet you at 7 o'clock, how can you be sure if they mean 7 o'clock in the evening or 7 o'clock in the morning? To make it clear they might add a.m. or p.m. The initials a.m. stand for 'ante meridiem', the Latin for 'before noon', and the initials p.m. stand for 'post meridiem', the Latin for 'after noon'. Another way to make it clear would be to use the twenty-four hour clock.

The twenty-four hour clock makes it easy to arrange times with people around the world – even if we don't speak the same language. This twenty-four hour clock was probably made in 1540 and is decorated with phases of the Moon.

Time-tables

A time-table is a quick and simple way of showing a lot of information about what will happen and when.

Time-tables help people to plan their journeys on buses, trains, coaches and planes. At this busy station, hundreds of trains arrive and depart every hour.

Here is part of a train time-table.

Searston	Boswich	Easlowe	Moretown
09.15	09.23	09.29	09.50
10.09	*	*	10.38
10.23	10.32	10.39	10.59
11.00	*	*	11.31

(* the train does not stop at this station)

Four trains leave Searston between 09.00 and 12.00. If you lived in Moretown, which train would you catch to arrive home before 10.50?

If you wanted to travel with a friend who had to get off at Easlowe, which train would you catch and be home on time? Which is the fastest train from Boswich to Moretown?

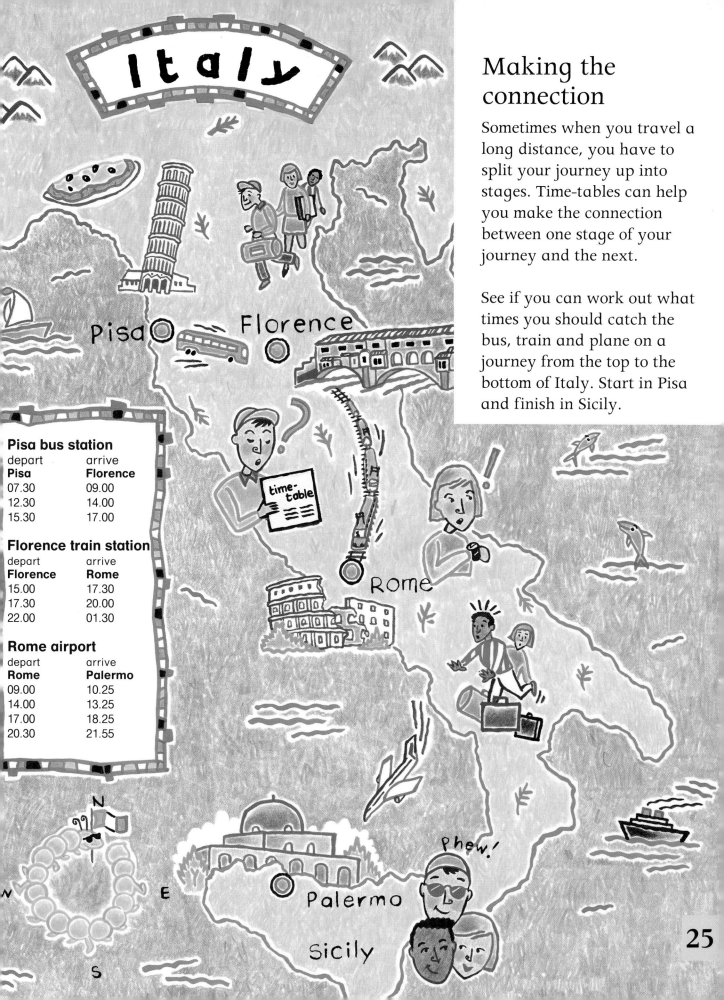

Italy

Making the connection

Sometimes when you travel a long distance, you have to split your journey up into stages. Time-tables can help you make the connection between one stage of your journey and the next.

See if you can work out what times you should catch the bus, train and plane on a journey from the top to the bottom of Italy. Start in Pisa and finish in Sicily.

Pisa bus station

depart	arrive
Pisa	**Florence**
07.30	09.00
12.30	14.00
15.30	17.00

Florence train station

depart	arrive
Florence	**Rome**
15.00	17.30
17.30	20.00
22.00	01.30

Rome airport

depart	arrive
Rome	**Palermo**
09.00	10.25
14.00	13.25
17.00	18.25
20.30	21.55

Time zones

As the Earth spins slowly, there is a constant series of dawns, noons and sunsets around the world. When people in the UK are eating lunch, it will be the middle of the night in California, and people in Japan will be getting ready to go to bed. Wherever people live, they use their own 'local time'.

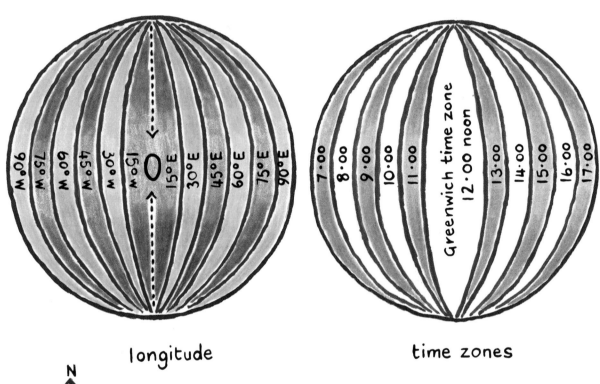

longitude

time zones

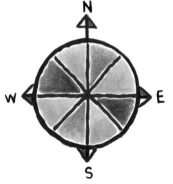

The world is divided into time zones and each has its own local time. The time zones are based on meridians, or lines of longitude. The world measures its time from the 0 meridian which runs through Greenwich, England. When you travel east and cross a time zone, you must put your watch forward, usually by one hour. When you travel west, you must put your watch back. Many countries have a single time zone, so watches are changed at the frontier, but large countries may be divided into a number of time zones.

The USA is such a big country it has four time zones; each is one hour apart from the next. The time zones are called the Pacific, Mountain, Central and Eastern Time zones. Some states are divided in two by a time zone.

On maps, one other line drawn along the Earth is the date line. The date line marks the place where a new day in the solar calendar begins. Most of the date line falls over the Pacific Ocean. Look up the date line in an atlas. On either side of the line the time is the same, but the date is different. If you travelled west from Los Angeles to Tokyo you would lose a day.

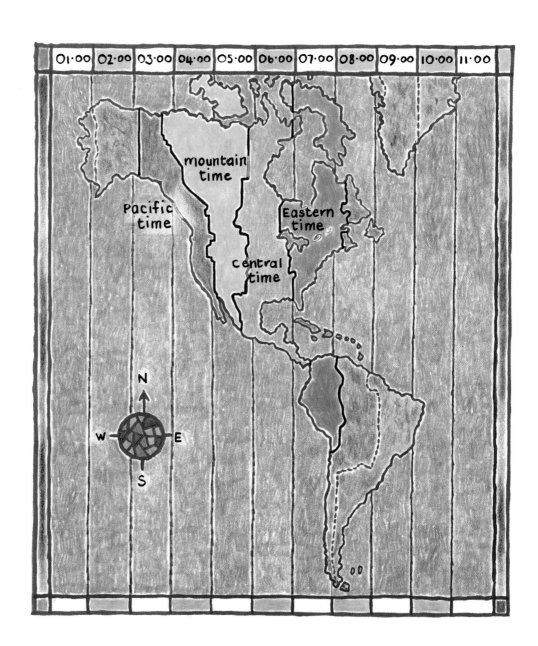

P.S. New Zealand is 12 hours ahead of London. India is 5 hours ahead of London. Greece is 2 hours ahead of London. When it's 10.00 in London, what time is it in New Zealand? When it's 09.00 in London, what time is it in India?

Dating things backwards

As people grow up, their appearance changes. You look very different from the way you did when you were a baby and your grandparents have changed a lot since they were your age.

Plants and animals change too. An acorn grows into a sapling and eventually becomes a huge oak tree. If you find an old tree which has been cut down, count the number of rings on its trunk. One ring grows for each year. When there's a drought, the tree won't grow very much and the ring will be narrow. But over a fine summer, a wide ring will grow on the trunk. How old was this tree when it was cut down?

Archaeologists study the way people lived many years ago. Sometimes when a new building is being built, the foundations of much older homes are discovered underneath. Remains of ancient buildings, tools and household objects can help to tell us how people used to live.

Scientists who study plants and animals that lived millions of years ago are called palaeontologists. They look at fossils, which are the remains of living things preserved in rocks. Palaeontologists can measure the amount of radioactivity in the fossils to see how old they are. This is called 'radio carbon dating'.

There are many ways of dating things. When do you think this photograph was taken? Photography was invented in 1850 so it must be after that date. It might be difficult to work out the exact date but there are plenty of clues. Look out for things which are different from today. For example what are the people wearing and what do you notice about the car?

Important events

4000 BC
The ancient Egyptians were probably the first to divide the day into hours. Before this, people divided the day into periods for different activities, such as sleeping, eating and farming.

2637 BC
The Chinese calendar starts. This is the year in which Emperor Huang Ti is thought to have invented the Chinese calendar.

2000 BC
Around this time, Stonehenge, in England, was built. This megalithic monument is made up of thirty upright stones connected by horizontal stones. It may have been used as a place to observe the Moon and stars.

1500 BC
Shadow-stick clocks were probably used as timekeepers in public places in Egypt. Water-clocks were used in Egypt and Greece.

46 BC
The Julian calendar, created by Julius Caesar's astronomers, was first used.

800–950
Viking invaders settle in Britain.

870
King Alfred is said to have invented the candle-clock.

1275
The first European mechanical clock was built in Burgundy, France, probably by a monk.

1475
The first clocks driven by coiled springs were made. They were easy to carry because they no longer had to be driven by a falling weight.

1492
Columbus's voyage west in search of the Spice Islands.

1582
Pope Gregory's calendar was first used. It is still in use today.

1584
Galileo observed a swinging chandelier in Pisa Cathedral, which led to the invention of the pendulum clock.

1657
The Dutch scientist Christian Huygens built the first pendulum clock.

1837–1901
Queen Victoria's reign.

1884
Greenwich Mean Time was adopted in most parts of the world, the standard time from which all the time zones were calculated.

1939–1945
Second World War.

1960s
The first quartz-driven clocks and watches were available.

More things to do

1 Page 12 If you want the water-clocks you made to measure longer or shorter periods of time, you could try using different sized containers, or make the hole in the bottom of the container or in the cap bigger or smaller.

2 Page 13 If you want to make a sand-clock that measures longer or shorter periods of time, you could use bigger or smaller bottles or make the size of the hole between the bottles bigger or smaller.

Some sand-clocks were made from several sand-clocks mounted in the same holder, a bit like a row of egg-timers. The first would time 5 minutes, the next 15 minutes and the next 30 minutes. Try this for yourself.

Candle-clocks will work for as long as there is wax left to burn. Compare a candle-clock made from a short fat candle and a long thin candle of the same weight. Which candle makes the better clock?

3 Here is a simple way to convert the time on the twenty-four hour clock to the time on the twelve hour clock. If the time is between 13.00 and 23.00 hours just take twelve away from the hour. For example 14.00 take away 12 is 2, which is 2pm, and 19.00 take away 12 is 7, which is 7pm.

4 The names of our months date from Roman times. July is named after Julius Caesar and August after Emperor Augustus. Try to find out how the other months were named.

5 As well as using clocks and watches, there are many other ways that people keep 'in time'. Watch a conductor beating time with a baton to help the musicians in an orchestra play together. A musician practising alone might use a metronome to keep a steady beat, and marching bands use the beat of a drum to keep in step.

6 Many public buildings have foundation stones, engraved with the year in which they were built. Some houses have plaques outside to tell you that a famous person lived there from a certain time. Look out for buildings with dates on them near to where you live.

7 People have always been fascinated by the possibility of travelling backwards and forwards in time. Have you read any stories or seen any films about time-travel? Write your own story about a time-machine that takes you into the future.

Index

First published 1992
A & C Black (Publishers) Limited
35 Bedford Row, London WC1R 4JH

ISBN 0–7136–3547 9

© 1992 A & C Black
   (Publishers) Limited

A CIP catalogue record for this book
is available from the British Library.

Acknowledgments
Photographs by Chris Fairclough,
except for: p3 (b), p24, p28, p29 (t) CFCL;
p4 NASA; p6 (t), p7 Ashley Holding
CFCL; p11 The trustees of Sir John
Soane's Museum; p12 (b), p13 (l), p15 (b)
Michael Holford; p16 (t) Bridgeman Art
Library; p19 Ian Robinson CFCL; p21
Graham Taylor CFCL; p22 (t) Martyn
Cattermole CFCL; p22 (b) Beamish Open
Air Museum; p23 Crown Copyright and
reproduced with the permission of the
controller of H.M.S.O.; p29 (b) John
Davies CFCL; main cover photo CFCL.

The author and publisher would like to
thank the staff and pupils of Thornhill
Primary School, and Rose Griffiths and
Alistair Ross for their help and advice.

Filmset by August Filmsetting,
Haydock, St Helens
Printed in Belgium by Proost
International Book Production